# My Own Scribbles!

Sowmya Santhosh

**Ukiyoto Publishing**

All global publishing rights are held by

**Ukiyoto Publishing**

Published in 2024

Content Copyright © Sowmya Santhosh

**ISBN 9789362693235**

*All rights reserved.*
*No part of this publication may be reproduced, transmitted, or stored in a retrieval system, in any form by any means, electronic, mechanical, photocopying, recording or otherwise, without the prior permission of the publisher.*

*The moral rights of the author have been asserted.*

*This is a work of fiction. Names, characters, businesses, places, events, locales, and incidents are either the products of the author's imagination or used in a fictitious manner. Any resemblance to actual persons, living or dead, or actual events is purely coincidental.*

*This book is sold subject to the condition that it shall not by way of trade or otherwise, be lent, resold, hired out or otherwise circulated, without the publisher's prior consent, in any form of binding or cover other than that in which it is published.*

**www.ukiyoto.com**

# Foreword

In the morning golden sun and the gentle rustle of autumn leaves, in the sweet dusky rains and starry skies, her poetry finds its voice, a voice that resonates deep within us, stirring emotions, and painting vibrant images of our innermost feelings. It is in these moments of quiet contemplation that she finds happiness, understanding, and a connection to something greater than herself.

In this collection of poems by my sister, Sowmya Santhosh, each verse is a journey, a reflection of her unique perspective on life, love, and the world that she sees and we often forget to see. Through her words, she invites us to see the beauty in the ordinary, to feel the depth of emotion in the simplest of moments, and to explore the complexities of the human experience.

As I read through these pages, I am reminded of the power of poetry to heal, to inspire, and to uplift. Each poem is a testament to my sister's talent and her ability to capture the essence of life in all its forms. I am honoured to introduce this collection of her poems and invite you to delve yourself into the world she has created, to feel the emotions that dance across the pages, and to be touched by the beauty of her words.

> Sowmya, the one dear, to my heart so near
> 
> Steps into the world of verses & words
> 
> I wish my talented little sister to cheer
> 
> All the way, as she takes over the worlds...

May these poems touch your heart as they have touched mine, and may you find joy, comfort, and inspiration in the verses that follow.

Warm regards,

Adv. Dr. Kriss Venugopal,

Author, Lawyer, Motivational Speaker, Actor and Voice Coach.

# Author's note in verses...

To my poetic muse, my husband who is so divine
A poet himself & in his goodness my words entwine
With his encouragement, my few words took flight
A tribute to him, love of my life, my soul's light.

Some casual woven responses to my brother's verses
A poetic dialogue of prompts transcending words
A dainty dance of emotions, a language of our hearts
Inked expressions, a tapestry of the bond of our souls.

Grateful to my niece, a budding poet with grace
Reads my verses, eyes in awe, gifts a sweet embrace
The days in the States, scribbling together at night
Were words full of encouragement so pure and bright.

To my younger brother, whose love, steadfast & true
Thank you for your sweet gesture which takes me through
My sister-in-law, a silent supporter of my endeavours
Parents, my strong pillars are my protective covers.

Million thanks to Raja & Bharat, my sweet dear kids
For letting me steal a few favourite songs from grids
To change lyrics and make my live shows a true hit
Thanks a ton, dears for remaining true to your spirit.

- Sowmya Santhosh

# Preface

My Own Scribbles is a collection of verses, a kaleidoscope of emotions, thoughts, experiences, feedback of prompts, and encouragements that make up my rhythm of life. Each one can be a snapshot of a moment, a feeling, a travelogue, devotion, love, gratitude, about loved ones or a resonation that has touched my heart and soul.

Poetry to me is not just a string of words, or something abstract, but simple and a lucid mirror that reflects the *depth* of my emotions and the richness of my experiences. You will find joy and sorrow, love and loss, all myriad shades and colours painted in these verses.

The themes explored here, are as diverse as life itself. From nature's beauty to the complexities of relationships, from quiet moments of introspection to the loud clamour of apprehension, each poem was a result of an inspiration, or an impression of my thoughts and perspectives. I am extremely grateful to all my motivators, influencers, and promotors who spurred me, and set me up in action otherwise this book wouldn't have seen the light.

I invite you all to embark on this journey, to immerse yourself in these scribbles of mine. Hold my hands as I take you from page after page. May these verses whisper to your soul and ignite the flame of imagination in you. Thank you.

My scribbles begin here with a few words
Like the tweet and chirps of morning birds
Take them into your heart or read them not
But there are the few lines, for you, I've got…

- Sowmya Santhosh

# Contents

| | |
|---|---|
| Smile | 2 |
| Spice box | 3 |
| A beautiful day | 4 |
| My happiness cove | 5 |
| Bangalore days | 6 |
| Smile of the Divine | 7 |
| Celestial marvel | 8 |
| Prompt | 9 |
| My cutie pie kunjunni | 10 |
| A prayer | 11 |
| Kite | 12 |
| Love | 13 |
| Circle | 14 |
| My Vibes | 15 |
| Garland of Love | 16 |
| My all-time Hero | 17 |
| Game of Choice | 18 |
| That dear one! | 19 |
| Morning Bliss! | 20 |
| Life is beautiful | 21 |
| Options | 22 |
| A wonder pill | 23 |
| Just a reminder | 24 |
| Guru | 25 |
| My Closet! | 26 |
| Feather on the crown! | 27 |
| My masterpiece | 28 |

| | |
|---|---|
| No identity | 29 |
| A gift from above | 30 |
| Dreams | 31 |
| Gratitude | 32 |
| Lion's share | 33 |
| Mind talk | 34 |
| A voice | 35 |
| A far away angel | 36 |
| Divine Protection | 37 |
| Signs so powerful | 38 |
| Happily, Ever after | 39 |
| My tale | 40 |
| Right or wrong | 41 |
| Your vibe | 42 |
| Ceremony | 43 |
| Angelic smile | 44 |
| Messenger of the Divine! | 45 |
| Memories so dear | 46 |
| Unborn | 47 |
| An everyday 10-minute tryst | 48 |
| Possessions | 49 |
| Myself | 50 |
| Priority | 51 |
| I'm happy today …everyday | 52 |
| Just for me yours lovingly | 53 |
| What I seek | 54 |
| Precious Times to hold in our hearts | 55 |
| Dad's Day | 56 |
| Café | 57 |

| | |
|---|---:|
| Worth the Wait! | 58 |
| Moonbow | 59 |
| Daughter's day | 60 |
| The Hidden Touch | 61 |
| Love is … | 62 |
| Beauty Sublime | 63 |
| Books | 64 |
| Mom | 65 |
| A beautiful soul | 66 |
| Shooting star - soulmate | 67 |
| An Angel in disguise… | 68 |
| Gratitude to my dear children… My illustrators | 70 |
| *About the Author* | *72* |

# Smile

A smile is a beautiful inbuilt accessory
Goes with any outfit, which is necessary
Better than any new piece of jewellery
Not a penny to lose, so wear it happily

A curve that adds thousand watts, all in one
A moment to multiply, be it old or young
Pass it on, wipe a tear, bring joy & cheer!
Life goes on, rolling down, now & here!

# Spice box

A portion of kindness I sprinkle on my way
A segment of my dear time to keep you gay
Whole container full of fondness overflows
A true compartment of care & your soul glows
A bowl of smiles, followed by song & dance
Miya flavour to your space, given a chance
My 5 spice box of uniqueness, at a glance!

# A Beautiful Day

The new day unfolds in its full vibrance...
Like peacock's feathers with all its brilliance
As the morning sun's rays fall on earth
I see a million happy faces; I know it's worth

Grey & white the colours of their uniform
Make them bright with smiles and in form
Lit up faces & giggles of sheer amusement
Fills my day, making it a true entertainment!

# My Happiness Cove

I look back at my gallery, my happiness cove
Lovely moments, fond memories, all in a row
Relive the joyous time, aid to lift your spirits
Thanks to google, my storehouse of cheers

Throwback memories, throw smiles back
Paint all pink, in the canvas of life so blank
Smile curves gleam to make good, the lack
All past clicks make us get back on track!

# Bangalore Days

Memories precious, ingrained forever
Moments together, priceless treasure
Music, movement & sky at its splendor
20 hours of travel, was lighter than ever!

# Smile of the Divine

How can I not smile when I hear a kirtan!
How can I not chant His name, my atman?
He is the anchor for all wandering minds
He is the cool shower for parched lands

# Celestial Marvel

Sun is always for the day

Lives, gives, spreads radiance to the Grey

Night, without the sun, goes astray

Can the moon and the stars replace him in anyway???

They are his mere reflections in some way

Sky moans craves yearns for that single ray

Which brings a rainbow in millions, a vibrant foreplay!!

But alas! Only the reflection of its brightness is left away

For the unlucky night is always at bay

On the other hand, the sun bestows its life and soul to the moon

Which takes the best part of him to cast

The most Tranquil restful gentle in form

Indeed, together is the finest transform

Which in turn makes their world so warm and calm.

# Prompt

May my reply line have a sweet slice
Sweeter than ever, a joyful spice
All I can share are some fond memories
Of us together, treading life's trajectories

It can be a drop to quench your thirst
A loving brook to swim in no haste
Soothing words for your ailing mind
A bit of comfort, sweetest of its kind

# My Cutie Pie Kunjunni

Seeing this teeny-weeny guy

Staring steadily at the sky ...

Inspires me to allow nature's peace ...

To give life, a new lease

# A prayer

How can I define myself?
A part of the Divine self
Moments of despair, when I pray
Millions of sparkles, you do spray
A soul in its path, a learning
Wean me off, while deviating!
On you I trust, with a whole heart
Let me down not, till I be your part!

# Kite

You are my gutsy kite, coloured white
Flying high, paving way for all who try
Ignoring the fighter kites, soaring in heights
Shifting & swooping, it's a spectacular sight

With the wind you move, not against
Teeny bit of love, is all you need to groove
Light at heart & you look so smart!
To bring your smiles, I can go extra miles!

# Love

Build no strong walls around you, let it flow
Keep no barricades, that will make you low
Love knows no bounds, no priority & option
Just feel it, never to come to a conclusion

I may be right, you may also be, who knows
Sensing your loved one's pain, known to souls
Lending an ear, a consoling word or do more
To lift a dear one crumbled down from the floor

## Circle

What's the beauty of a mere circle?
Choice of the sun as seamless curve
Shape of the ring, binding a couple
The silver moon with the gleam of love

Is it the fullness, an attraction to enso?
Imperfection & impermanence, is it so?
Circle of togetherness, the nature of life
Live it, love it, light it up, not just survive.

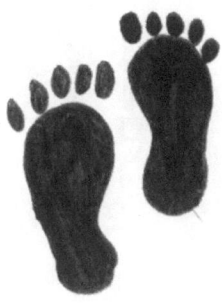

# My Vibes

Today, like all days let the world feel my vibe
Brimming with smiles, spread amidst my tribe
Bring a change if my presence can, I'll stay
Let my absence leave a footprint, I do pray

# Garland of Love

Love which cannot be expressed with full heart
A fear to loom, scenes from my forgotten past
Picking flowers one by one, with due care I string
A garland of love, with all colours of the spring!
My hands are tied, as petals may go shriveled
My love untied, never to end up, just withered

# My all-time Hero

Who is the super hero of your book?
Is he the one who made you look
Within you, with all fervour to seek
The answers, all around you, do sneak

The one who is with you, always to care
Hold his hand leave him not, He's so dear
No frills or tags attached, go ahead, just dare
To keep him in the loop and in your prayer

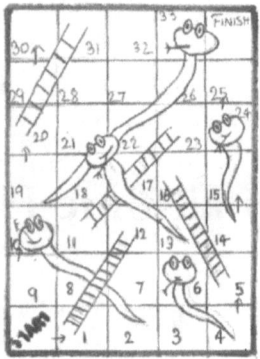

# Game of Choice

Snake & ladders, a game for kids, my favourite
Didn't know the significance, much later realized it
Fascinated by the hues & shapes, rewards & pitfall
Rolled the dice, I moved with an excitement overall

The journey of life, a similar game, to reach the number
Aiming at hundred, with the goal of getting a true bumper
Not to fall prey to the snake, risk taken on each move
Ladder of knowledge to ascend, keeping all in the groove!

# That dear one!

Thoughts forlorn, travel far & wide
Energy impulses felt profound, swell
Dear one's care towering as a shade
"What happened", words sounded well

Be it a silly strain, or a trivial pain
A call from the One, won't go vain!
To lift me up from the rift, He'd strain
Ripples of laughter then pour as rain!

# Morning Bliss!

The rays of the morning sun ignite my spirit

The lines of your poem add to the credit!

Filling our battered hearts with inspiration

All positive words to make the day a celebration!

# Life is beautiful

Life is a beautiful journey, our route in fortitude
Filling our days with purpose, kindness & gratitude,
Let's do or dare, the hitches & catches we embrace
Moving towards a smile and a positive phrase…

# Options

To be the significant one, in someone's abode
Vulnerable is it, if that someone leaves, bored
Not to meet the waterloo, but to become invincible
Priority is you, others be the options, no trouble.

# A wonder pill

Greenery I see all around, carpeting Mother Earth
Vast blue sky, a cozy warm blanket, know it's worth,
Covering the green rock in whole, smiling with mirth
Isn't this a panacea for all the minds' silly dearth?

Gratitude, a lingering thought, I'd choose to say
It's an elixir for peace, keeping conflicts at bay
A wonder pill of joy, a bubbling stream, so to say
To ward off pain, to turn today in a magical way

## Just a reminder

Surrounded & covered by the pods are peas
Enveloped & protected are we by God's grace
In each living being who dare to see the truth
A reminder for all, a care to sail across smooth

A cabbie who takes me to my destination
A stranger he is, picks me up from the station
Late night or day, my fears to be kept at bay
I've peace within, faith where it all does begin

# Guru

Than the best of all, you are more!
I always wish I had met you before...
Safe & joyful I am in your presence
Mindful I be in the sheer sweet silence
Can it be taken away by distance?
Isn't love in the heart, the essence?


You taught me never to succumb
When life ahead has a hump & bump
Imparted in me, the true "Song of God "
To lead life, righteous against all odd

## My Closet!

Colour your thoughts with what you put on
Dress yourself in warmth, smiles to add on
Shades of pink, hues of love, a tinge of kindness
All in one outfit, bringing a dazzle of goodness

Clothe yourself with grace & gratefulness
Accessorize with empathy & happiness
Be it a normal day or a special occasion
Choose to wear it, never go out of fashion

# Feather on the crown!

Rambling down the lane, one day,
I saw a spectacular sight!
Peacocks dancing around, out in the open,
feathers so bright
I saw Him, Most beautiful work of the creator,
a marvel in itself
No wonder it's so special, it's feather worn by
Lord Krishna himself

A true symbol of purity, a symbol of His love
and of gratitude too
What else do I need if I can be a feather on
His crown, of the few?
Just the sight of it drives me to strive hard
with the right attitude
To be with the Lord, in his abode,
as a part of His own, in fortitude…

# My masterpiece

Am I an artist, am I painting my own masterpiece?
What are the colours I would choose to appease?
Will I give the brush to someone else to perfectly fix?
Or Will I be happy with my own created sketchy mix?

Let it be messy, let it be clumsy, I'd just laugh at them
I make mistakes, make wrong choices, yet I own them
I stumble and fall, I rise again and walk tall, grace it is
That guiding hand of His, His love & light never to miss!

# No identity

Hunger to live invisible in this visible world
Doing good deeds, not get hurt, being bold
Hunger to learn & explore more, free-willed
In a life befitting a true devotee, spirits unfurled

# A gift from above

Each day a wrapped gift box, what it bore
Though we don't know what it has in store.
Carry your smile, and pure thoughts within
Savour this very moment, colour it sanguine

# Dreams

Dreams have wings which make us fly
Wishes are dreams to His abode, high
Compassion & love keep me on the float
Virtues to adhere in life I do make a note

Given solace and happiness with pure heart
I have done my best, even when I am apart
Now I seek for something higher, a purpose
I search for omens, from beings so righteous

# Gratitude

I am enough, I am grateful
Let me let go of perfections
Embrace life's true lessons
I am that I am, I'm beautiful

What comes to me, His grace
As blessings I take, I do face
Not competing with anyone
Just relying on the Supreme One

# Lion's share

With all goodness of heart, I share
With all sweetness of thought I care
Be it a lion's share or just a teeny bit
Adding some love & smiles, I never quit

Right & wrong, good & bad, I don't know
Melting heart for the loved ones though
In the path I choose, I walk steady but slow
Surrendering to God & I go with the flow

## Mind talk

It can be silly, or blatantly childish
Who cares, let it be, it's your wish
Things you do, does matter to you
With all love & pomp, you would do

Silly it can be, but my kitten teaches
Valuable lessons that a person ignores
Sprinkle some silliness in life, my way
Smiles to go with, throughout the day

# A voice

Countless stars in the sky, a visual treat
Boundless love in the heart, felt in a beat
Radiating all around you, unfettered as care
Bringing a lot of smiles, with blessings you dare!

You are in a world, me in another, destined to
Meet together, changing me to a person new
Hand in hand, and a prayer to lead me forth
From inside me, a voice of love & warmth!

# A far away angel

Am I not fortunate to have found you ...?
What did I do in my previous births, no clue
Plentiful blessings from heaven showered on me!!
All through an angel, lighting up my face with glee!!

# Divine Protection

If my smile can make the mountains move

If my spark can make ailing heart groove

If my energy, my love can heal your mind

If my light can send all your worries behind

I happily send all my good vibes, to wipe tears,

Your way, to bring you bliss and cheers!

# Signs so powerful

The taste of tears makes the drops of joy sweeter...
Delve deep within, the lessons learnt make us wiser ...
Experience both, beyond the dark realms of fear...
Divine hands, protect us from all and take us near ...
Angelic signs, leads to the purpose, this birth does bear
Doors open, to show us the life path so clear!

# Happily, Ever after

Is 'forever' a lie? Does nothing last forever?
Everything changes, paves the way for another
Good time does pass, so does troubles & woes
Why brood and lose happy times, life shows

Have trust the pilot, the omniscient divine self
Who takes us through life, safe, all by Himself
Be it dark stormy weather, paths rough or tough
With prayers as the fuel we sail, that's enough…

# My tale

My tale is the one, I should only know
No fault finding eyes, no poking nose
I learn from my errors & I take it slow
No one can walk the journey, though

The guidance of the Divine through my loved one
Is all I need to make my lore a beautiful one
Fragrance of a dew, smiles of those trusted few
Paint my path, pink &white all heavenly hues

# Right or wrong

Is it right to make your happiness a priority?
Is it selfish or self-care, I need to give clarity
Charge your batteries with all zest and zeal
Nothing like self-care, gives that happy feel
Load yourself with more love, joy and glee
Then serve others what you have in plenty!

## Your vibe

Your smile is like the gushing waterfall
Bringing torrents of joy in the minds of all
Your talk is as gentle as the mountain streams
Flowing with all goodness of the plains & valleys
Painting my day with all colours of joy & love
What more I need as a blessing from above
Other than a cozy hug loaded with care, a fond wish too
And few words spoken in the Divine language of love
true!

# Ceremony

To cut red ribbons tied, using the scissors no harm
To sever some bonds, use your power as your charm
To enter a new world, guilt free & take your testimony
Let this be the day for that, the inaugural ceremony…

Walk in with head held high, holding your loved ones
Who are your armour, nevertheless your true saviours
Away from the clasps of ruthless, lifting all the barriers
Living a life befitting a queen, being forever righteous!

# Angelic smile

Where can I find an angel, to my heart so dearest?
Is she amidst the array of the tall trees in the forest?
Where can I find an angel, who heals my wounds & burns?
Is she in the Ganges, floating on the twists and turns?
Where can I find an angel, even when I know not how?
Is she seen among the fluffy creamy clouds up above?
Where can I find an angel, who has no end or start?
Is she dwelling in us as love, in each one's heart?
Where can I find an angel, whom I search all the while?
Is she reflecting as a piece of art, in our true smile?
Where can I find an angel, who has no hue of guile?
Is she flowing, as soothing words, from our Isle?
Where can I find an angel? Does anyone know today
Is she waiting for me, or to her, paving me the way…

# Messenger of the Divine!

Ignore your loved one, you will regret
You won't meet another one, don't fret
You have one, God sent to love & care
Taking him for granted, a gem so rare…

Feel the pain, feel the aches he endures
Lend an ear, a text, a few loving moments
Far or near, he yearns to hear, the voice
Of his own, nothing else enough to rejoice!

# Memories so dear

Memories of the day so fond, linger in all
Like the dew on the leaf reluctant to fall
Colours I see of the morning sun, hidden
In the droplet, ready to merge in the billion

A dew drop's whisper, within me I can hear
Today I am near, tomorrow I may not be here
Come & see what I have in store, with glee
Let those stay in you, and sorrows & fears flee

# Unborn

"Am I the luckiest one?" I asked myself
"Or His pet, His favourite?" I asked life
Makes even my unborn thoughts a reality
Silly wishes as well, simple yet with clarity

What's waiting for me unborn I pay no heed
What's born & needs care and prayer I feed
Unborn, I leave to Divine, to do the needful
Dwelling on the blessed moments so joyful

# An everyday 10-minute tryst

No one is ever born in this world to love
No one will ever be born again to live
A lifetime & more, loving a soul, but how
Not bound by time, but to gently give

Into a world of yours, to rock n roll & more
Fortunate or unfortunate I don't know
For that was her destiny, to swiftly go…
And I see you, waiting to end the show...

# Possessions

A dream I saw today,
Of late, makes me take away
The cover of helplessness,
To drape on me awareness
I had forgotten my diamonds,
And I kept running after trinkets
Piling them one after the other,
Leaving my real jewels suffer…

The day came with a halo & smiles
Seemed to disperse the trinket piles
To toss the Knick- knack obsessions
And I see again my priced possessions
"Blessed me", with what I have, I realized
The Valued Divine, with a halo, I recognized!

## Myself

How can I define myself?
A part of the Divine self
Moments of despair, when I pray
Millions of sparkles, I see thee spray

A soul in its path, learning
Wean me off, while deviating!
On you I trust, with whole heart
Let me down not, till I be your part!

# **Priority**

Life is a beautiful journey, our route in fortitude
Filling our days with purpose, kindness & gratitude,
Let's do or dare, the hitches & catches we embrace
Moving towards a smile & a simple positive phrase ...

To be the significant one in someone's abode
Vulnerable is it, if that someone leaves to adore
Not to meet the waterloo, but to become invincible
Priority is you, others be the options, no trouble.

# I'm Happy Today...
# Everyday

A cool morning, on a cozy bed, I woke up today
Texted good morning to my loved one, far away
Stepped in for a wash, no time for the bathtub waiting
For me to soak in the warm water, or indulge in relaxing

Adorned in my new garb, ready to explore Ho Chi Minh
Off to the breakfast hall, sumptuous spread, no sin!
Something a rarity now, with my kin I sit to eat
What more do I need, these few moments so sweet!

# Just For Me Yours Lovingly

A star shines on you today with a wish
That your life changes on a wand's swish
One among the stars born on this earth
To be shaped again in life's hot hearth...

# What I seek

I lost my dear Krishna somewhere...
Don't know how to search, or where...
His love, those sweet words & laughter
Spins my world, it's most sought after!!!

He created magic through his voice
Like Bansuri, his tunes captivated all!
Sharing his smiles through verses all the way
And his good deeds share, made my day

# Precious Times to hold in our hearts

Moments to memories, we travel along
Loved ones to hold, for there I belong
With utmost care the bonds were made
Left behind with some snaps and shade

I worry not for whatever lost, let it be
I bury them for good as I believe in thee
Before me a door to the garden lay open
And a basket of blessings for the season

# Dad's Day

Sweet Smiles are his signature
His sweet talks always add a spur
A family man, so true to his word
Complaints from him, never heard!

# Café

An interesting place, a cozy Café, ready to greet
Well lit, around the corner of a busy bustling street,
Freshly brewed coffee, so tempting I couldn't resist
Ordered one, a Vietnam special, so did they insist…

"Are they here for a drink or for chit chat ", I wondered
Rattling along, forgetting all around, as if nothing mattered
Laughter & giggles seemed to blend with the music playing
Serious talks too paved way for something truly amazing!

# Worth the Wait!

Waiting can be sweet, waiting can be pain
Sometimes it can be worthless and in vain
Waiting, it does take away our precious time
At times it brings loads of glories and chime
Waiting is worth every moment of it, I'd say
For the blessed celestial star may make us gay!
Showing up at the right time and in my prime
Making hay while the sky does sparkle in time
My waiting, eager longing, is for Him to appear
To shower His blessings on us, leave us in cheer!
Love these celestial beings who just love us more
Vast blue sky, Shining stars, Sun & Moon, mi amor
Who know to give without asking & nothing more?
And make us smile from within, with prayers galore!

# Moonbow

I see you as my moonbow, sent by the angel
Even in the darkness deep, it gleams on me, so gentle
As a smiling arc of faith you say - I 'm there!
Sending encouraging messages & You do care!
Not all can see that mysterious celestial being
Coz it's God 's gift for special ones, with a touch of healing
An enigma to some, a sensation to many
To me, the end of my search for a divine fairy
Moonbow, a rare phenomenon, but it's real
Treasure trove, full of rare wisdom, you are ideal!
Clueless to find an apt catchphrase for You
Adjectives fall off, feeling so deficient seeing You!

# Daughter's day

A day of celebration, a day for daughters
Just for social media or for the good era?
For those who have, the blessed lot, I'd say
For those who don't, be a part of the party

"Take that chain out, not suiting" says one
Calls of care, "where are you" & day is done
"Short hair is better" and takes to the parlour
Daughters' love, trigger to live, an armour!

# The Hidden Touch

I am a joyous being, a love-filled soul
Do I really need to rely on others for all?
The power within me, makes me whole
Grateful for what I have, big and small!

Within each one of us, we've a Midas touch
Opens all the doors, which were shut, such
Even a smile can do wonders, give it a try
Brings to you a golden glow, take it high!!

# Love is ...

Few beats of love, and beats of care
Fairy wings to take me high, when I dare
Loved ones around to hold your hand
Always secured with the magic hand
God's love is to be felt inside, I know that
Self -love is nothing less than that!
Along with love comes prayers which shields you
Along with love comes respect and good energy too
Along with love there is trust, support, and harmony
Acceptance to some, space & boundary for many!
Love is all… all is love & nothing matters more
That's a lesson about love, I've learnt more…

# Beauty Sublime

Your verse is so beautiful with the loving beads
That we cherish in our treasure cove as heart beats
You thread each word with purity, a pristine expression
Carefully presented to us as a fond note of affection!!

The way you thread the sweet words together
Strewn to be a beautiful garland, verses to jingle!!
Gently with all your love and care, you do gather
Joyfully touching our hearts to shine & twinkle!!

## Books

Books are indeed the treasure coves
Paradise for the readers, word troves
Unfold a whole new world, beyond ages
Take a leap into the thoughtful pages

Stories, fiction, mystery, folklore & more
Fairies, super-heroes, goblins and more
Countries far & wide we can see and feel
Through the books, without moving a heel!

# Mom

My mom's sermons, they seem so endless
Her tensions, about me, are so boundless
Her care, drenched in love, is so limitless
Her protective words, filled with coziness
She's not a mom who hugs and embraces
Neither she's expressive in words or gestures
But for her, her whole wide world is just us ...
I always adore her, she is strong and sensible
I admire her, her brawn, the way she's flexible
She always remains my role model, by all means
I am her loving daughter, by God Almighty's grace!!

## A Beautiful Soul

Devoted her life, not a part, but whole
But never used any words that cajole
Stood for us, as a true supporting soul

Her protective words are our armour
Enamoured with love & care, a charmer!
With her, the world seems soothingly warmer

Not with hugs or embraces, she expresses
But with caution & concern, she converses
Strong, sensible, tender at heart, still impresses

Her brawn & flexibility, inspires, goes heart ward!
You showed me the bright light, the outer world
But to you, we are your light, the entire world!

# Shooting star - soulmate

While reading a book, a thought did pop
For wandering minds, a shelter to stop
Connection of souls, instant or karmic?
Finding a soul, destined by the cosmic?

Like a shooting star, a flicker on the skies
Bringing good luck, to the believers, the wise
Brightening up our lives, soulmates enter
Heartening up our spirits, so we surrender

A soulmate does open the doors untold
For that divine purpose, a path to unfold
A positive spark, close, it brings us all
A silver streak, to readily awaken our goal

A loving Midas touch, and lo! We glow!
Once mission accomplished, they part & go

# An Angel in disguise…

Your good morning wish brings an instant smile
And I float in happiness for a good long while
Your quick call lifts my spirits up, makes me bright!
And I fly up in the sky, flapping my wings in delight!

A voice with all tenderness calms my mind like a
prayer
Evoking feelings of loving kindness, all around the air
Busy schedules, hectic work don't stop you from care
God given trait of yours, for righteous things you
dare!

You keep no records of wrongs, no excuses to tug on,
Accepting the ones who love you, with all flaws on,
Never go back in promise, neither hurt me nor
ignore!
With all fondness and awe, I look upon you and more

With gratitude I count you, blessings galore
Wish fulfilling angel, nurturing to the core
With small loving gestures, you bring colours
Smile on you never fade, that makes my prayers…

# Gratitude to my dear children… My illustrators

These lines are not just for expressing gratitude to my young illustrators who, out of their passion for art, readily agreed to sketch apt illustrations for my poems, but also to promote the talents of the next generations who are highly creative and blessed with talent. I acknowledge and appreciate their efforts who were indeed young artists with great minds!

Thank you, my dear students!

Dhanya Sri

Sreemathi

Nithin

Abijith

Gunan

Sibe Chakravarthi

Thank you PKD family, who have embraced me with all kindness and warmth, I take a moment to express my gratitude to all the budding poets of the School who have started exploring the realms of poetry. They capture thoughts, observations and emotions, journaling them in their notes following their curiosity and creativity! Hats off my little ones!

I extend my heartfelt thanks to all my Lakshmi School staff, colleagues, students, and friends especially Ms. Shanti Mohan, Sr. Principal, Lakshmi School, Ms. Uma Ramanan, Principal, Disha A Life School, Ms. Geetha Balachandran, VP, Lakshmi School, Ms. Navya, Coordinator, Lakshmi School, Ms. Selvi Santhosham, Admin Head, LVS and Ms. Mythili, Director of LVS, from LVS family for nurturing and bringing out the best in me!

Poetry under the stars, a unique programme at Lakshmi School made me scribe a few poems to recite along with the students in front of an August gathering.

# About the Author

**Sowmya Santhosh**

Sowmya Santhosh, a passionate educator, with specialized training in creative teaching methods, and an innovator with more than ten years of experience fostering a positive and inclusive learning environment. Committed and dedicated leader promoting academic, social and emotional growth in students and the teaching community.

Academic Head of P.K.D. Matric Higher Secondary School with a Masters in Applied Psychology, certified Dyslexic trainer & Dance Movement Therapist. A trained classical dancer currently pursuing Mural Arts, Kathak, Mohiniyattom and singing. My passion for the language helped me to co-author a textbook and activity books, and compose songs and rhymes on theme-based Curriculum for Primary Kids.

www.ingramcontent.com/pod-product-compliance
Lightning Source LLC
LaVergne TN
LVHW041540070526
838199LV00046B/1758